SPORTING CHAMPIONSHIPS
Stanley Cup

Blaine Wiseman

WEIGL PUBLISHERS INC.
"Creating Inspired Learning"
www.weigl.com

Published by Weigl Publishers Inc.
350 5th Avenue, 59th Floor
New York, NY 10118

Website: www.weigl.com

Library of Congress Cataloging-in-Publication Data

Wiseman, Blaine.
 Stanley Cup / Blaine Wiseman.
     p. cm. -- (Sporting championships)
 Includes index.
 ISBN 978-1-61690-127-1 (hardcover : alk. paper) -- ISBN 978-1-61690-128-8 (softcover : alk. paper) -- ISBN 978-1-61690-129-5 (e-book)
 1. Stanley Cup (Hockey) I. Title.
 GV847.7.W58 2011
 796.962'648--dc22

                              2010006164

Printed in the United States of America in North Mankato, Minnesota
1 2 3 4 5 6 7 8 9 0 14 13 12 11 10

052010
WEP264000

Weigl acknowledges Getty Images as its primary image supplier for this title.

Project Coordinator
Heather C. Hudak

Design
Terry Paulhus

All of the Internet URLs given in the book were valid at the time of publication. However, due to the dynamic nature of the Internet, some addresses may have changed, or sites may have ceased to exist since publication. While the author and publisher regret any inconvenience this may cause readers, no responsibility for any such changes can be accepted by either the author or the publisher.

Every reasonable effort has been made to trace ownership and to obtain permission to reprint copyright material. The publishers would be pleased to have any errors or omissions brought to their attention so that they may be corrected in subsequent printings.

CONTENTS

24

What is the Stanley Cup?

The Stanley Cup is the most important trophy in hockey and the oldest professional sports trophy in North America. Standing at 2.94 feet (0.90 meters) tall, and weighing 34.5 pounds (15.7 kilograms), the shining silver cup is one of the best-known sights in hockey. Presented each year to the National Hockey League (NHL) champion, it is one of the most difficult sporting trophies to win.

The NHL is made up of 30 teams from across North America. It is the best-known hockey league in the world, and it attracts the most talented hockey players. Each team plays 82 games during the regular season, which runs from October until April. After the regular season, the top eight teams from each **conference** play in the Stanley Cup playoffs. By June, one team has the honor of hoisting the Stanley Cup.

Many Stanley Cup champions start playing hockey at a young age. Pittsburgh Penguins captain and 2009 Stanley Cup champion, Sidney Crosby, started playing hockey at two years of age.

CHANGES THROUGHOUT THE YEARS

Past	Present
In 1892, Lord Stanley of Preston bought the cup for 10 **guineas**. This was less than $50.	Today, the Stanley Cup is considered priceless to millions of hockey fans and is **insured** for more than $1 million.
The original Stanley Cup was only 7.28 inches (18.5 centimeters) tall.	The cup has grown to more than three times its original size.
Players and coaches of the 1907 Montreal Wanderers were the first to engrave their names on the Stanley Cup. A total of 20 names were put on the cup.	In 2009, the Pittsburgh Penguins won the cup. Team members' names were added to the cup, bringing the total number of names on the cup to 2,163.

The Trophy

The Stanley Cup is the only trophy in team sports that displays the names of every winner. Each year, the Stanley Cup winning team is allowed to have the names of 52 members added to the rings of the cup. This can include players, coaches, management, and staff. Due to this **tradition**, the cup has grown over the years, with pieces being added so that more names could be engraved. Every 13 years, a section of names is removed and placed on the wall at the Hockey Hall of Fame in Toronto, Canada. The section is replaced, so there will be room for new winners. In this way, the Stanley Cup continues its tradition of displaying the names of champions.

Stanley Cup History

In 1892, Sir Frederick Arthur Stanley, Lord Stanley of Preston, purchased a silver bowl from a shop in London, England. Stanley was Canada's governor general and a hockey fan. The cup was first presented in 1893 to the Montreal Amateur Athletic Association (MAAA). The team had won a **tournament** called the Dominion Hockey Challenge. Later, the event would become known as the Stanley Cup. Montreal won the tournament again the following year and many more times since. The NHL's Montreal Canadiens have won the cup a record 24 times. No city has won more Stanley Cup championships.

In 1915, two hockey leagues decided that, each year, the best team from the Pacific Coast Hockey Association (PCHA) in the West would play the eastern National Hockey Association (NHA) champion. In 1916, the NHA's Montreal Canadiens defeated the Portland Rosebuds of the PCHA for their first Stanley Cup championship. The next season, Montreal challenged the Seattle Metropolitans. The Metropolitans won the four-game series three games to one at home in Seattle. They became the first U.S. team to win the Stanley Cup.

GET CONNECTED
You can learn all about every Stanley Cup final at **www.legendsofhockey.net**.

Montreal won the Stanley Cup in December 1895.

The following season, the NHA was replaced by the NHL. It was 1917, and five teams competed for the NHL championship. The team that came to be known as the Toronto Arenas won. Later, the Arenas challenged the PCHA champion, the Vancouver Millionaires, for the Stanley Cup title. Toronto won the five game series three games to two. They became the first NHL team to win the Stanley Cup.

The Vancouver Millionaires played against the Ottawa Senators in the 1915 Stanley Cup playoffs. The Millionaires won the best of five series in three games.

In 1926, the NHL's Montreal Maroons defeated the Victoria Cougars for the cup. After this, the Stanley Cup became the official championship trophy of the NHL. Since then, only NHL teams could win the cup.

Nels Stewart of the Montreal Maroons scored six goals in four games during the 1926 Stanley Cup playoffs.

Rules of the Game

Hockey is a rough, fast sport. Players are allowed to use their bodies to knock down other players who have the puck. The Stanley Cup playoffs are considered a different season, compared to the NHL regular season, because the games are set up as a tournament.

1 The Game

An NHL playoff game is made up of three 20-minute periods. There is an intermission between each period so that an ice-cleaning machine, often called a Zamboni, can make the ice smooth again. At the end of the game, the team that has scored the most goals wins.

2 In the Zone

The rink is divided into three separate zones. They are the neutral zone, the offensive zone, and the defensive zone. The neutral zone is in the middle, between the two blue lines. Center ice is marked by a red line and the faceoff circle. The offensive and defensive zones are end zones, and they are at opposite ends of the ice. There are nine faceoff dots spread around the ice. Every time the game is stopped for a goal, penalty, **offside**, or any other reason, it is restarted at the appropriate faceoff dot. The neutral zone contains five dots, while each end zone has two.

3 Beginning the Game

A hockey game begins with a faceoff. The teams line up on each side of the faceoff dot. The referee drops the puck between the two centermen, who try to get the puck to one of their wingers or defensemen.

4 Overtime

During the playoffs, the NHL uses a continuous "sudden death" overtime system. This means that if the score is tied after three periods, the teams continue playing 20-minute periods until one of the teams scores. The first team to score in overtime wins the game. Stanley Cup overtime play can be the most exciting action in hockey.

5 Penalties

If a player breaks a rule, he is given a penalty. Minor penalties include cross-checking and hooking. Players who are given a minor penalty sit in the penalty box for two minutes. The team plays with one less player during this time. A major penalty, such as fighting, is a five-minute penalty. A player who receives a **misconduct** penalty can spend 10 minutes in the penalty box and can also be thrown out of the game.

Making the Call

NHL games are refereed by a team of officials. Their job is to make sure teams are playing by the rules. There are two referees and two linesmen. Referees wear orange bands around their arms so that they are not confused with linesmen. Referees are in charge of the game. They stop the play any time a rule is broken. Referees watch the play and call penalties when a player breaks the rules. Linesmen are in charge of calling offsides and **icing**. They also break up fights.

The Hockey Rink

A hockey rink is made up of a large sheet of ice with a net at each end. High boards surround the ice. The floor underneath the ice is painted with lines and circles that can be seen through the ice. A thick red line is placed in the middle of the ice, and there are two thin red lines near the ends. Two blue lines are painted between the red lines.

The Road to the Cup

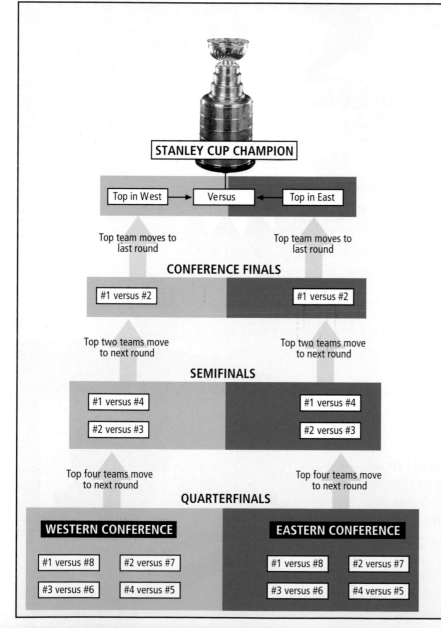

STANLEY CUP CHAMPION

Top in West → Versus ← Top in East

Top team moves to last round

Top team moves to last round

CONFERENCE FINALS

#1 versus #2

#1 versus #2

Top two teams move to next round

Top two teams move to next round

SEMIFINALS

#1 versus #4

#2 versus #3

#1 versus #4

#2 versus #3

Top four teams move to next round

Top four teams move to next round

QUARTERFINALS

WESTERN CONFERENCE

#1 versus #8   #2 versus #7
#3 versus #6   #4 versus #5

EASTERN CONFERENCE

#1 versus #8   #2 versus #7
#3 versus #6   #4 versus #5

There are currently 30 teams in the National Hockey League. Half of the teams play in the Eastern Conference. The other half play in the Western Conference.

Eight teams from each conference advance from the regular season to the playoffs. Playoff spots in the conference quarterfinals are awarded on the basis of points earned during the regular season. Teams are **seeded** from #1 to #8 based on their regular-season points. Four series are then played with #1 playing #8, #2 playing #7, and so on. Each series is a **best-of-seven** format. The first team to win four games wins the series.

The winners of the conference quarterfinals advance to the conference semifinals. The winning teams are seeded in each series based on the same criteria as the quarterfinals. Winners of the semifinal series then advance to the conference finals. Conference winners play each other for the Stanley Cup.

The boards around the rink are designed to keep the puck and players inside. There is usually glass or wire mesh that sits on top of the boards. This keeps the puck from flying out and hitting people in the stands. There are benches for the players of each team to sit on. Special gates at the benches allow players to go on and off the ice easily. As well, there are two penalty boxes where players go when they break the rules.

The Hockey Rink

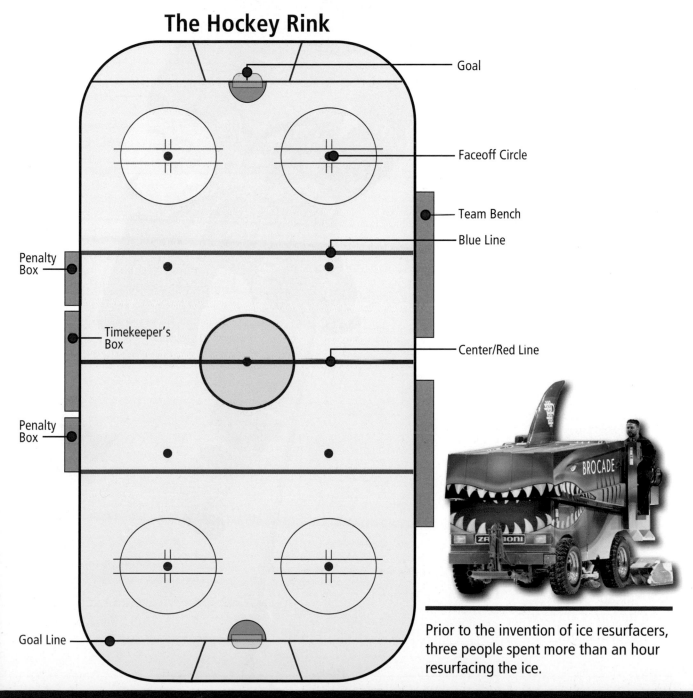

Goal

Faceoff Circle

Team Bench

Blue Line

Penalty Box

Timekeeper's Box

Center/Red Line

Penalty Box

Goal Line

Prior to the invention of ice resurfacers, three people spent more than an hour resurfacing the ice.

Hockey Equipment

Helmet

Jersey

Gloves

Skates

Stick

Hockey injuries are common because of the fast, physical nature of the sport. Players wear special equipment that helps protect them from injuries and allows them to play their best.

Players skate around the rink, crashing into each other and slamming into the boards and the ice. It is important that they protect their head from injury. Made of hard plastic and foam padding, helmets protect players from head injuries. The NHL and other leagues around the world are working on reducing the risk of head injuries to players through rule changes.

GET CONNECTED
Learn all about hockey team uniforms at **www. nhluniforms.com**.

Instead of a ball, hockey uses a round, flat disc called a puck. The puck is made of solid rubber and can be shot at more than 100 miles (160 kilometers) per hour. Pucks are 1 inch (2.54 cm) thick, 3 inches (7.62 cm) in diameter, and weigh 5 ounces (142 grams). Although pucks are small, they can break the glass surrounding the rink or players' bones. For this reason, players wear padding on almost every part of their body. This allows players to stand in front of **slap shots** with less chance of receiving a serious injury.

Hockey skates are advanced equipment that allow players to glide across the ice. The boot offers ankle support and padding. It keeps the player safe from ankle injuries, such as sprains and strains, as well as impact injuries caused by fast-moving pucks.

Players move the puck around the ice using hockey sticks. These special pieces of equipment can be made of wood or more lightweight materials, such as fiberglass, carbon fiber, or graphite. The blade of the stick is usually curved, which helps players raise the puck off the ice.

In 1920, the average player was 5 feet 9 inches (1.75 meters) tall. Today, players such as Mike Fisher stand an average of 6 feet 1 inch (1.85 m) tall.

Uniforms

Each hockey team wears its own uniform so it can be distinguished by the players, officials, and fans. All members of a team wear matching jerseys, pants, socks, gloves, and helmets. Teams customize their uniforms with a unique logo and color scheme. Each player wears a jersey with his team's logo on the front. The player's name and number are on the back of the jersey. The number is also on each sleeve. Teams have three sets of uniforms. One is mostly white, with team colors used as an accent. The second mainly features the team colors. The third is used for special occasions, such as the first home game of the year. In the NHL, the home team chooses which of its uniforms it will wear during the game. Usually, a team chooses to wear its darker jersey, which shows the team colors more clearly.

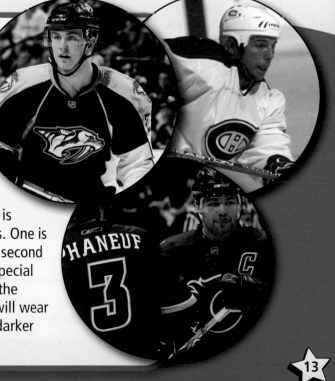

Qualifying to Play

The quest for the Stanley Cup begins with the NHL preseason. Teams play a series of **exhibition games** before the regular season. These games are like a training camp, in which players try out for the team. By the end of the tenth regular season game, each team chooses which players will be on the team for the remainder of the season.

The regular season is made up of 82 games for each team. The teams play 41 games at home and 41 games away from home, traveling to different cities to play against other teams. The teams travel all over North America. Some even begin the season playing in Europe. The travel schedule can be tiring.

Teams must try to gain as many points as possible during the regular season to qualify for the playoffs. A win is worth two points, while a loss in overtime or a shootout is worth one point.

Hockey players from around the world join NHL teams to compete for the cup. Alexei Kovalev came to North America from Russia to play in the NHL. In 1994, he won the Stanley Cup with the New York Rangers.

Hockey has many fans in the United States. The Stanley Cup finals can draw millions of fans to watch a single game on television.

At the end of the regular season, the top eight teams from each conference qualify for the playoffs. Each team that qualifies for the Stanley Cup playoffs is matched up against another team for the first round, with the winner advancing.

In total, a Stanley Cup champion must survive the preseason and 82 regular season games. After that, teams must play four best-of-seven rounds and win at least 16 playoff games.

Hairy Superstition

During the Stanley Cup playoffs, players have a tradition of growing long facial hair. Many hockey players are **superstitious** and feel that they have a better chance of winning the cup if they have a long beard. It is considered bad luck to shave during the playoffs. By the time a team wins the cup, most players on the team have thick beards and moustaches.

Where They Play

It takes about 15,000 gallons (56,781 liters) of water to create the ice surface of an NHL hockey rink.

The Stanley Cup playoffs are the biggest annual event in the hockey world. Each spring, 16 cities across North America have the opportunity to host the playoffs. As teams advance through each round of the playoffs, their cities become more excited. The excitement builds until one city can celebrate its team's Stanley Cup championship.

In 2004, the Calgary Flames qualified for the playoffs for the first time in eight seasons. That year, the tradition of the "C of Red" began. Fans packed the local arena, wearing red to support their home team.

Stanley Cup Champions 2000–2009			
Year	Champion	Runner-Up	Series
2009	Pittsburgh Penguins	Detroit Red Wings	4–3
2008	Detroit Red Wings	Pittsburgh Penguins	4–2
2007	Anaheim Ducks	Ottawa Senators	4–1
2006	Carolina Hurricanes	Edmonton Oilers	4–3
2005	No Championship		
2004	Tampa Bay Lightning	Calgary Flames	4–3
2003	New Jersey Devil	Anaheim Ducks	4–3
2002	Detroit Red Wings	Carolina Hurricanes	4–1
2001	Colorado Avalanche	New Jersey Devils	4–3
2000	New Jersey Devils	Dallas Stars	4–2

After each game, as the Flames advanced to game seven of the finals, 60,000 fans dressed in red would gather on a street nicknamed "The Red Mile" to celebrate their team's success.

Other teams enjoy different playoff traditions. In Detroit, octopi from local sea food stores are traditionally thrown onto the ice during playoff games. Often, teams host parties for their fans when the team is playing away from home during the finals. In 2009, the Pittsburgh Penguins hosted **tailgate parties** outside of Mellon Arena when the team was playing in Detroit against the Red Wings.

The championship city traditionally holds a Stanley Cup parade to celebrate its team. The team rides through the city, showing off the cup. Fans pack the streets to catch a glimpse of the Stanley Cup and the champions.

As many as 375,000 fans came to cheer on the Penguins in downtown Pittsburgh after their 2009 Stanley Cup victory.

Places the Stanley Cup has Visited

The Stanley Cup has traveled around the world with players of the winning team. This map shows just a few of the places the cup has visited.

1905
Having just won the Stanley Cup, a Silver Seven player said he could kick it over Ottawa's Rideau Canal. His kick was short, and the cup landed in the middle of the frozen canal.

1986
Montreal Canadien Chris Nilan took a picture of his son sitting in the cup.

NORTH AMERICA

OTTAWA
MONTREAL
PITTSBURGH
NEW YORK
WASHINGTON

PACIFIC OCEAN

ATLANTIC OCEAN

1994
Ed Olczyk of the New York Rangers brought the cup to the Belmont racetrack in New York so the 1994 Kentucky Derby winning horse could eat from it.

SOUTH AMERICA

1999
Pittsburgh Penguin Mario Lemieux left the cup at the bottom of his swimming pool.

2009
When Pittsburgh Penguins captain Sidney Crosby went to the White House to meet President Obama, he brought the cup with him.

SOUTHERN OCEAN

Legend

Continents

Oceans

Places the Stanley Cup has visited

621 Miles

0   1,000 Kilometers

N
W   E
S

ORNSKOLDSVIK

MOSCOW

LONDON

PRAGUE

ASIA

EUROPE

AFRICA

PACIFIC OCEAN

1996
The cup visited a European player's home for the first time when Colorado Avalanche player Peter Forsberg brought it to his hometown, Ornskoldsvik, Sweden.

1997
Detroit Red Wings players Slava Fetisov, Slava Kozlov, and Igor Larinov took the cup to Moscow.

1999
Roman Turek of the Dallas Stars took the cup to Ceske Budejovice, which lies 100 miles (160 km) south of Prague, to show it in the town square.

INDIAN OCEAN

AUSTRALIA

1892
Lord Stanley of Preston purchased the cup in London, England.

Women and the Stanley Cup

Women have been playing hockey for more than 100 years. While women's hockey has been gaining popularity over the past 10 years, only one woman has ever played in the NHL. Manon Rheaume played in goal for the Tampa Bay Lightning for one exhibition game in 1992 and one in 1993.

The top female hockey players are highly skilled. There are excellent women's leagues in the United States, Canada, and several European countries, such as Sweden and Finland. In these leagues, women compete against each other in a similar format to the NHL.

In 2005, the Stanley Cup was not awarded in the NHL because of the **lockout**. The governor general of Canada wanted to award the cup to the top women's team instead. The plan was not popular. The commissioner of the National Women's Hockey League believed the cup belonged to men's hockey champions. Instead, the Clarkson Cup was created. The cup was named for Canadian Governor General Adrienne Clarkson.

GET CONNECTED
Visit **www.whockey. com** to learn more about women's hockey around the world.

The first Clarkson Cup was awarded to Team Canada after its gold medal win at the 2006 Winter Olympics in Turin, Italy. Today, the top four women's hockey teams in North America compete for the cup at the end of each hockey season.

Even though a female player has never won the Stanley Cup, there are women who have become cup champions and had their names added to the legendary honor roll. In 1954, Marguerite Norris became the first woman to have her name engraved on the cup when she was president of the champion Detroit Red Wings. Norris' name also appeared the following year when the Red Wings became champions again.

Four women share the record for having their names on the cup more than any other women, and they all come from the same family. In 1997, 1998, 2002, and 2008, the names Marian Ilitch, Denise Ilitch Lites, Lisa Ilitch Murray, and Carole Ilitch were engraved on the cup as owners of the Red Wings.

Canada has won the most Olympic gold medals in women's hockey.

Olympics

The most popular tournament in women's hockey takes place at the Winter Olympics every four years. Women's hockey has become one of the most-watched events at the Winter Olympics. The United States and Canada have been the two most powerful teams. They played each other for gold in 1998, 2002, and 2010. Team USA won the first women's Olympic hockey gold medal in Nagano, Japan, in 1998. Canada won the next two times they faced the United States for gold, in 2002 and 2010. In 2006, Canada won gold against Sweden.

Historical Highlights

There are misspellings and incorrect names on the cup that have never been corrected.

Throughout the history of the Stanley Cup, there have been many notable moments. Some are remembered for being exciting, while others have been tragic.

In the 1904 to 1905 season, the Dawson City Klondikers, a team made up of **gold prospectors**, left the Yukon Territory to challenge the Ottawa Silver Seven for the cup. The Klondikers traveled by bicycle, train, boat, and even dogsled on a 25-day trip that covered more than 4,000 miles (6,437 km). The Silver Seven were the defending Stanley Cup champions. Only one day after arriving in Ottawa, the team from the Yukon lost to "One Eyed" Frank McGee and the Silver Seven by a score of 9 to 2. The second game was even worse for the Klondikers. McGee scored a Stanley Cup record 14 goals, and the Silver Seven won 23 to 2.

During the 1951 Stanley Cup, the Toronto Maple Leafs led their rival, the Montreal Canadiens, three games to one in the final series. With the score tied at two goals in game five, Bill Barilko scored a goal two minutes and 53 seconds into overtime to win the cup for the Leafs. It would be his last goal. That summer, during a fishing trip in northern Canada, Barilko was killed in a plane crash. The Maple Leafs did not win another Stanley Cup until the wreckage of the plane crash, and Barilko's body, were found 11 years later, in 1962.

Hockey players and fans consider the Stanley Cup the ultimate team trophy. No player can win the cup without getting help from his teammates. Sometimes, however, one player becomes the focus of the entire series. In 2001, Ray Bourque joined the Colorado Avalanche after a 21-year career with the Boston Bruins. Bourque had won five Norris trophies as the league's best defenseman. He had become one of the greatest players of all-time, but he had never won the Stanley Cup. The Avalanche hoped to help Bourque end his career by becoming a champion. The Avalanche faced the defending champions, the New Jersey Devils, who they defeated in a seven-game final series.

It has become a Stanley Cup tradition for the captain of the winning team to hoist the trophy over his head before passing it to other team members. Colorado captain Joe Sakic went against tradition. After he was awarded the cup, Sakic handed it to Bourque, allowing the Hall of Fame defender to hoist the cup.

Ray Bourque holds the NHL records for most goals, assists, and points by a defenseman.

Stanley Cup Playoff Records		
Record	Player	Team
Stanley Cups (11)	Henri Richard	Montreal Canadiens 1956-60, '65, '66, '68, '69, '71, '73
Career goals (122)	Wayne Gretzky	Edmonton Oilers, Los Angeles Kings, St. Louis Blues, New York Rangers
Career points (382)	Wayne Gretzky	Edmonton Oilers, Los Angeles Kings, St. Louis Blues, New York Rangers
Career games played (366)	Chris Chelios	Montreal Canadiens, Chicago Blackhawks, Detroit Red Wings
Most goals in one year (19)	Reggie Leach Jari Kurri	Philadelphia Flyers 1976 Edmonton Oilers 1985
Most points in one year (47)	Wayne Gretzky	Edmonton Oilers 1985

LEGENDS and Current Stars

Wayne Gretzky

Wayne Gretzky is one of the best players in hockey history. When he retired from the NHL in 1999, Gretzky had won four Stanley Cups and owned more than 60 NHL records. Gretzky first came into the league in 1979. It was also the first year in the NHL for the Edmonton Oilers. Gretzky led the league in scoring and helped the Oilers qualify for their first playoffs. Gretzky and the Oilers were a major force in hockey in the 1980s, winning the Stanley Cup in 1984, 1985, 1987, and 1988. Gretzky was awarded the Conn Smythe trophy as playoff MVP in 1985 and 1988. His playoff records include the most goals, assists, points, game-winning goals, and **hat tricks**.

Maurice Richard

Maurice "The Rocket" Richard is the best-known Montreal Canadien in history. He was one of the best players of his generation. Richard won a total of eight Stanley Cups with the Canadiens. In 1952, he scored the cup-winning goal in game seven with blood running down his face from an injury. Richard was the first player to score 50 goals in a single season and the first to score 500 goals in his career. Richard's final game was game four of the 1960 Stanley Cup finals. The Canadiens **swept** the Toronto Maple Leafs.

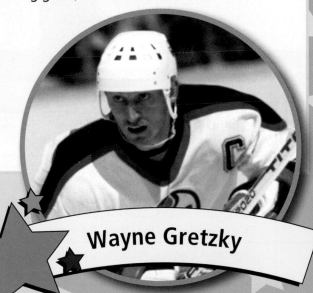

Wayne Gretzky

Sidney Crosby

In 2008, Sidney Crosby became the youngest captain ever to lead a team to the Stanley Cup finals. He was only 20 years old. That year, Crosby and the Pittsburgh Penguins were up against the Detroit Red Wings for the cup. Although they lost in six games, Crosby and his team had another chance to win the next year. The 2009 final was a rematch, with the Penguins and Red Wings again facing each other. The series was one of the most exciting in recent history, with the Penguins winning game seven by a score of 2 to 1. Crosby had 15 goals in the playoffs to lead the league. With 31 points, he finished second in playoff scoring behind his teammate, Evgeni Malkin. At 21 years old, Crosby became the youngest captain to win the cup.

Nicklas Lidstrom

Sidney Crosby

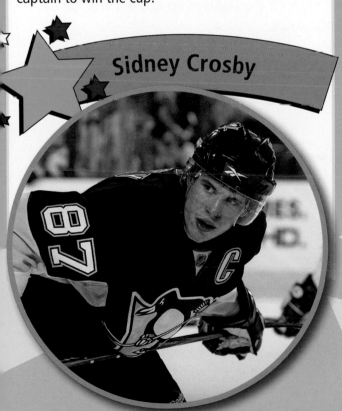

Nicklas Lidstrom

Since the mid-1990s, the Detroit Red Wings have been the most successful team in the NHL. There have been many players who have helped the Red Wings become a great team. One of these players is Nicklas Lidstrom, who took over as team captain when Steve Yzerman retired. Lidstrom has won four Stanley Cups with the Red Wings. He has also won six Norris trophies as the league's top defenseman. In 2008, the Red Wings defeated the Penguins for their 11th championship, the most of any U.S. NHL team. Lidstrom became the first European captain to lead his team to the Stanley Cup. Lidstrom is one of the most consistent defensive players in NHL history. Considered the best Swedish defenseman of all-time, Lidstrom is a Stanley Cup and Norris trophy contender every year.

Famous Firsts

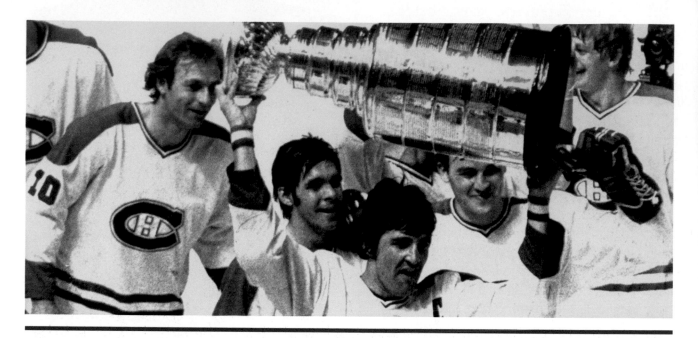

The last time two of the original six NHL teams faced each other for the Stanley Cup was in 1979. The Montreal Canadiens beat the New York Rangers four games to one.

In 1924, the Montreal Canadiens defeated the Calgary Tigers to win their second Stanley Cup. Following their win, the Canadiens started one of the greatest traditions in sports. They added the names of all the team members to the cup. Since 1924, every team that has won the cup has engraved its members' names on Lord Stanley's Cup.

The first time the Stanley Cup finals were televised was in 1953. The Canadian Broadcasting Corporation (CBC) covered the series in English. Danny Gallivan called the play-by-play as Montreal defeated Boston in five games. The series was broadcast in French by René Lecavalier of SRC, the French branch of the CBC.

Mark Messier is the only NHL player to lead two different teams to championships as captain.

In 1988, the Edmonton Oilers won their fourth Stanley Cup in five years. After their victory lap with the cup, the players, coaches, management, and staff gathered on the ice for a picture with the trophy. The team came together in a pile, with the cup in front. This began the tradition of taking the championship team photo on the ice after the final game.

The Stanley Cup is the most traveled trophy in sports. Every year, each member of the winning team gets to spend one day with the cup, showing it off to family and friends. The cup is accompanied on trips by its official **guardian**, known as "White Gloves." Many players have taken the cup home through the years, but in 1995, the New Jersey Devils were the first team to take part in this official tradition. The cup has climbed mountains, visited foreign countries, and been used as a cereal bowl. In 2009, photos showed Sidney Crosby sleeping with his arms around the trophy.

There is only one Stanley Cup that travels. It has a symbol on the bottom to prove it is the real cup. It can be seen when the cup is lifted.

The First Stanley Cup

The Stanley Cup was first awarded in 1893 after a short tournament involving five teams, three of which were from Montreal. The Montreal AAA won by finishing the eight-game Dominion Challenge with a record of seven wins and one loss. The AAAs allowed only 18 goals in the tournament. They defeated the Ottawa Generals 2 to 1 in the final game to win the first-ever Stanley Cup championship.

The Rise of the Cup

1892

Lord Stanley of Preston buys the cup.

1893

The Stanley Cup is awarded to the Montreal AAA.

1916

The Seattle Metropolitans become the first U.S. team to win the cup.

1917

The Toronto Arenas become the first NHL team to win the cup in the league's first year of existence.

1924

The NHL takes over as guardian of the Stanley Cup.

1927

Teams begin adding narrow rings to the bottom of the original bowl so they can engrave their names on the cup. By 1947, the cup is known as the "Stove Pipe Cup."

1942

The Toronto Maple Leafs defeat the Detroit Red Wings in game seven of the first Stanley Cup finals.

2009

Sidney Crosby becomes the youngest captain to win the cup.

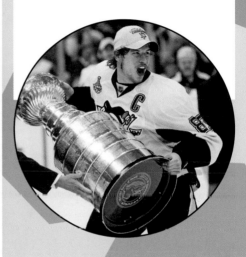

1993

The Montreal Canadiens win their 23rd Stanley Cup in the NHL and 24th overall in the trophy's 100th year.

1947

A wide base is added to the cup.

1970

The original Stanley Cup is retired to the Hockey Hall of Fame. It is only removed to be presented to new champions.

2008

Nicklas Lidstrom becomes the first European captain to win the Stanley Cup.

QUICK FACTS

- Of the 30 teams in the NHL, 13 have never won the Stanley Cup.

- The Stanley Cup has been awarded every year since 1893, except 1919 and 2005. In 1919, the tournament was started, but a flu outbreak prevented a winner from being determined. There was no 2005 Stanley Cup playoff because the season was canceled due to a lockout.

Test Your Knowledge

1 Which team won the first Stanley Cup?

2 How much does the cup weigh?

3 How is a hockey game started?

4 What are the three zones of a hockey rink?

5 How many playoff games must a team win to become Stanley Cup champions?

6 Which player has won the most Stanley Cups?

7 Who scored his last goal in overtime to win the 1951 Stanley Cup?

8 When were the Stanley Cup finals first televised?

9 What U.S. team has won the most Stanley Cups?

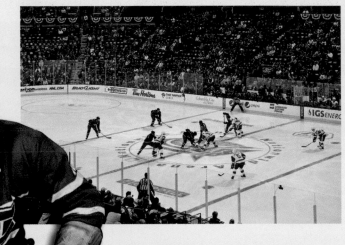

10 Who scored 14 goals in game two of the 1905 Stanley Cup challenge?

ANSWERS: 1) Montreal AAA 2) 34.5 pounds (15.7 kg) 3) With a faceoff 4) Neutral, offensive, and defensive 5) 16 6) Henri Richard with 11 7) Bill Barilko 8) 1953 9) The Detroit Red Wings (11) 10) "One Eyed" Frank McGee of the Ottawa Silver Seven

Further Research

There is more information about the Stanley Cup and hockey available on websites and in books. To learn more about the Stanley Cup, visit your library, or look online.

Books to Read

Search your library for books about the Stanley Cup. On your library's computer, type in a keyword. The computer will help find information you are looking for. You can also ask a librarian for help.

Online Sites

The National Hockey League website contains a great deal of information about the history of the Stanley Cup. Check out this website at www.nhl.com/cup/fun_facts.html

Learn all about the names on the cup by visiting www.hhof.com/legendsofhockey/html/silver_stFFFs.htm

To read the Stanley Cup journals to see where the cup is traveling next, visit www.hhof.com/html/exscj_main.shtml

Glossary

best-of-seven: a seven-game series in which the first team to win four games wins the series

conference: the NHL is divided into the Eastern and Western conferences, with 15 teams in each

exhibition games: games that do not affect a team's ability to win the cup

gold prospectors: people who look for gold deposits or gold mines

guardian: the person or organization who looks after the Stanley Cup

guineas: gold coins used in Great Britain starting in 1663; they are no longer used

hat tricks: when players score three goals in a single game

icing: when a player shoots the puck all the way down the ice from his own side of the center line

insured: protected against loss, damage, or theft

lockout: when an NHL season had to be canceled because the players and owners could not agree on salary contracts

misconduct: punishment for behaving poorly

offside: when an attacking player enters the offensive zone before the puck

seeded: being placed in a specific rank or position

slap shots: the hardest shots in hockey

superstitious: believing something that is not based on reason or knowledge

swept: when a team has won a best-of-seven series in four straight games

tailgate parties: parties in the parking lot of an arena where people bring their own food and barbeques

tournament: a series of matches between a number of teams competing for a prize

tradition: an act based on established practice or belief

Index